CLASSIC ROCK CLIMBS
NUMBER 18

CASTLE CRAGS

CALIFORNIA

by
Laird Davis

CHOCKSTONE

FALCON®

HELENA, MONTANA

A FALCON GUIDE®

Falcon® Publishing is continually expanding its list of recreation guidebooks. All books include detailed descriptions, accurate maps, and all the information necessary for enjoyable trips. You can order extra copies of this book and get information and prices for other Falcon® guidebooks by writing Falcon, P.O. Box 1718, Helena, MT 59624 or calling toll free 1-800-582-2665. Also, please ask for a free copy of our current catalog. Visit our website at www.falconguide.com

DEDICATION

This book is dedicated to the climbing pioneers of Castle Crags, those who stood first upon the virgin spires and those who continue to establish new routes. Their routes are masterpieces painted upon the domes and spires. Taking turns on the sharp end, belaying, and supporting each other, they toiled under a hot dry sun and shivered in the chill of dark north faces. Their creations are in harmony with the environment and were done for the noblest of reasons; they love the crags and they love to climb. They're not famous and you won't read about their exploits in the climbing journals.

They are my heroes and I follow in their footsteps (and handholds) with deep appreciation and humility.

And to Tad Craig for his generous bounty of friendship, support, and spirit.

TABLE OF CONTENTS

Tad Craig on the summit of The Ogre.
Photo: Laird Davis.

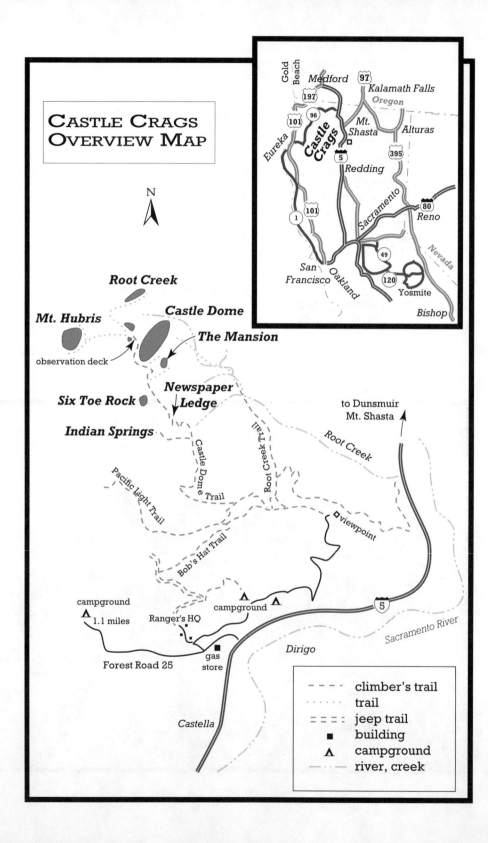

INTRODUCTION

CASTLE CRAGS
CALIFORNIA

Rock-climbing, as such, should be accepted with the greatest enthusiasm; yet I feel that certain values should be preserved in our contact with the mountains. While it is rarely a case of the complete ascendancy of acrobatics over esthetics, we should bear in mind that the mountains are more to us than a mere proving-ground of strength and alert skills.

— Ansel Adams, 1931

Castle Crags Wilderness is part of the Shasta National Forest, located in northern California between the towns of Dunsmuir and Castella. When viewed from afar, the spires and domes burst forth from the forested hills, invoking an image of castles-in-the-sky.

Even though the area is easily accessed from Interstate 5, climbing here is essentially a backcountry experience. While some climbs can be approached in under an hour, most require at least a four- to five-mile roundtrip hike that can take up to four hours. For the most part, the approach is a pleasant stroll through a pristine wilderness until you get closer to your objective. Here you can expect scrambles in steep gullies and bushwhacks through manzanita bushes.

There are no "sport" climbs in the wilderness; old-fashioned trad climbing is the order of the day. Top-roping is not an option. If you want to climb a route in Castle Crags, you have to lead it, utilizing a traditional rack for protection. Although there are a few good cracks, the majority of routes are face climbs in the 5.6 to 5.10 range. Most are from one to six pitches in length. While the more dangerous cruxes are often bolt protected, most routes are serious undertakings—this is not the place to push yourself into a higher grade. If you want to climb a 5.10 route, you need to be a solid 5.10 leader and be comfortable with long runouts on the easier terrain.

The Shasta area is predominantly volcanic and sedimentary rock with granite plutons that formed during the Jurassic period. Castle Crags, subsequently sculpted by glaciers, is one of these plutons. Because the rock is relatively young, exfoliation—the peeling and crumbling of the outer surface—is still prevalent. Expect good rock on the established routes and poor rock elsewhere. The highest quality rock is found on routes that follow dikes and watercourses.

HISTORY   Modoc Indians were the original inhabitants of the area. They regarded the spires with awe and superstition, rarely venturing to the higher elevations. Their economy was based on Pond Lily seeds as their main staple, supplemented by hunting and fishing. Accomplished weavers, they lived a peaceful existence until the arrival of the gold-seeking white man in the mid 1800s. Modoc resistance to the immigrant encroachment climaxed in the 1855 Battle of Castle Crags, which marked the beginning of the long Modoc War and the end of the tribe's sovereignty. By 1864 their population had dwindled to 250 survivors.

Joaquin Miller "The Poet of the Sierras," guided people up nearby Mt. Shasta in the early 1850s. Joaquin worked for "Mountain Joe," one of General Freemont's men. In addition to climbing Mt. Shasta and perpetrating the myth of lost Indian gold, he led parties into the Crags, leaving wooden tablets on some of the mountain tops with dates and names carved into them.

For climbers, the Crags have been a fabled and mysterious place. Post-war explorers of the '40s and '50s climbed most of the peaks by easy third- and fourth-class routes. The Hoyt brothers, William and Fletcher, climbed most of the larger formations by obvious routes. The Stanford Alpine Club was instrumental in the early development of the area. One of America's early rock stars, John Harlin II, was a member of the club and helped introduce technical climbing to the area. Allen Steck was among the first of the modern era climbers to make the pilgrimage in hopes of putting up first ascents on Yosemite-type walls. Other famous names rumored to have climbed here include Pratt, Harding, and Lowe. What they found was less-than-perfect rock and few cracks to hammer their pitons into. A few classics and some forgettable routes were put up and the area was largely ignored. Shasta locals, namely Michael Zanger, Bob Rears, Jerry Sublett, and Bill and John Weiland, continued to develop the Crags. The '70s and '80s brought a new breed of climber more interested in hard free routes. They boldly ventured onto the faces, sparsely bolting 5.10 cruxes with a hand drill while on the lead. Active in this time were Byron Cross, Peter Chesko, John Bald, Stan Miller and Tim Loughlin.

CLIMATE   At an average elevation of 4000 feet, Castle Crags enjoys a temperate and dry climate. The climbing season extends from mid-spring to mid-fall. Although summer temperatures can top 100°, thermal breezes make the climbing enjoyable.

FLORA AND FAUNA   Trees of the area range from live oak in the lower elevations to red fir, Jeffery pine and weeping spruce near the Crags summit. Mixed conifer forests include western yew, Port Orford cedar, incense cedar, sugar pine, ponderosa pine, Douglas fir, white fir and lodgepole pine. Broadleaf trees such as big leaf maple, vine maple, black oak and Pacific dogwood can be found in the area.

The area contains over 300 varieties of herbaceous wildflowers. Indian rhubarb, tiger lily, pitcher plant and yellow monkey flower can be found in the moist areas. The Castle Crags hairbell (*Campanula shetleri*) is a flower found only in the Crags. Poison oak is also common at lower elevations.

Birds of the wilderness include jays, ravens, warblers and other common woodland species. Hawks, golden eagles and peregrine falcons are also known to inhabit the area.

Reptiles common to the area are lizards and rattlesnakes. Although the local variety of rattlesnake (*Crotalis viridis*) is neither as poisonous nor aggressive as the southern variety, caution is advised.

Mammals include the common ground squirrel, gray squirrel, coyote, mule deer, bobcat, mountain lion and black bear.

PRECAUTIONS AND REGULATIONS   To access the Castle Crags Wilderness, it is necessary to park and begin your approach hike in the Castle Crags State Park. A $5 day-use fee will be collected at the entrance to the park. There is no water available in the climbing areas. Climbers should take at least two quarts of water per person; more in hotter weather. Water is available at Indian Springs, 200 yards off the Castle Dome Trail, but that's still a mile away from Castle Dome.

This is bear country. Take the necessary precautions, especially when camping in the backcountry.

GEAR AND SPECIAL NEEDS   A standard rack of nuts and cams, augmented with micro-nuts and extra TCUs should suffice for most climbs. Take ten quickdraws and six slings. Also take a knife and extra webbing to insure that the fixed belays and rap anchors are safe since many of the routes see few ascents. Carry a headlamp for the inevitable slog back to the car in the dark.

RATINGS   The Yosemite Decimal System is used to rate the difficulty of the climbs. A star rating system has been used in an attempt to rate the quality of a route. If a route does not get a star rating, it can mean one of two things: either it is of poor quality—not worth climbing, or that the author was unable to determine the quality of the route. Factors that determine the quality of a route include: rock quality, quality of protection and belays, sustained for its grade, aesthetics of the route, and ease of approach and descent.

★   A good route, worth hiking two hours to climb.

★★   An excellent route, as good as you will find at any other climbing area.

★★★   The best of the best. A route you'll remember 20 years after you climb it.

EMERGENCY   In case of emergency, contact the Ranger office located at the entrance to the park. If the office is closed, drive down the road toward I5 and call 911 from the service station located at the highway exit.

GETTING THERE   The Castle Crags are located .5 mile from I-5, 10 minutes south of Mt. Shasta City and an hour north of Redding. There is an obvious exit for Castle Crags State Park off of the Interstate (sorry, but the exits are not numbered). The approach trail leaves from the scenic overlook inside the state park. It gains 1500 feet of elevation on the 2.5 mile approach. The approach trail is easy to moderate and takes from 1.5 to 2 hours. This trail, which goes to the top of Castle Dome, is also the descent route for all of the Castle Dome climbs.

CAMPING ACCOMMODATIONS   Camping is available at the State Park located adjacent to Interstate 5. The fee is $12 in the off-season (mid-fall to mid-spring) and $15 for peak season and holidays. The sites are on a first-come, first-served basis. Running water and hot showers are included. Because the Crags reside within Shasta National Forest, which is separate from the park, backcountry camping is allowed among the spires and domes. Check with the rangers for fire permits. For a small fee the rangers will allow you to park your car overnight in the park.

A medley of lodging is available in Dunsmuir and the town of Mt. Shasta. In Dunsmuir, check out the Dunsmuir Inn Bed and Breakfast, located in the center of town on Dunsmuir Avenue.

FOOD, COFFEE, SHOPPING   No visit to the Crags is complete without a visit to Dunsmuir, five minutes from the state park. Take Dunsmuir Avenue into downtown and head for the train station, located one block east of city center on Sacramento Avenue. Across the street from the station is a refurbished area featuring funky shops and restaurants. There is even a movie theater in town.

After bagging a route, dinner at the Rostel Pub and Cafe is mandatory. The Cafe Maddalena, Nutglade Station Coffee Shop, and Gary's Pizza Factory are all excellent. In Mt. Shasta, look for the climber's coffee shop; Has Beans on Mt. Shasta Blvd.

GUIDE SERVICES AND EQUIPMENT STORES   The Fifth Season, located in downtown Mt. Shasta City at 300 N. Mt. Shasta Blvd., (916 926-3606) is a complete source for equipment and information.
The Shasta Mountain Guides (916 926-3117) know the Crags better than anyone else and are also available to guide the climbing and skiing on nearby Mt. Shasta.

HOW TO USE THIS BOOK   All of the climbs in this book are in the vicinity of the Castle Dome Trail. The climbs are listed in the order that they are encountered as you hike from the Viewpoint parking lot up into the Crags.

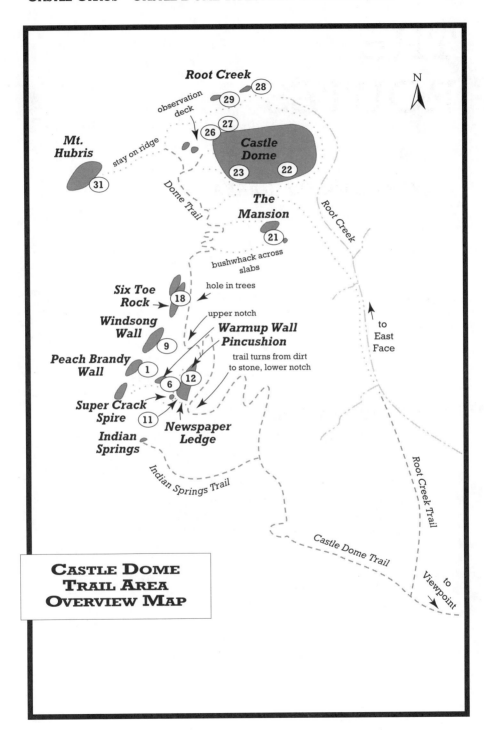

Root Creek

N

observation
deck

stay on ridge

**Mt.
Hubris**

31

29   28

26   27

**Castle
Dome**

23   22

Root Creek

Dome Trail

**The
Mansion**

21

bushwhack across
slabs

hole in trees

**Six Toe
Rock**   18

upper notch

**Warmup Wall
Pincushion**

to
East
Face

**Windsong
Wall**   9

trail turns from dirt
to stone, lower notch

**Peach Brandy
Wall**   1

6   12

**Super Crack
Spire**   11

**Newspaper
Ledge**

**Indian
Springs**

Indian Springs Trail

Root Creek Trail

Castle Dome Trail

to
Viewpoint

**CASTLE DOME
TRAIL AREA
OVERVIEW MAP**

THE ROUTES

CASTLE DOME TRAIL AREA

Indian Springs is the first area encountered on the Castle Dome Trail. Located 100 yards above Indian Springs, the area is a mixed bag of short routes. The climbing here is not remarkable. The routes have been included because of their easy access and the fact that they offer the only top-roping possibilities in the park.

APPROACH   *Park in the state park at the Viewpoint parking lot. From the parking lot, follow the Castle Dome Trail for 2 miles, at which point it turns from smooth dirt to rocky steps. At the apex of a sharp right-hand turn, in the vicinity of the first rock encountered, look for a faint climber's trail that leads up and to the left. Follow the trail for 50 feet, then scramble up slabs to the right to gain Newspaper Ledge. Approach time: 60 minutes.*

PEACH BRANDY WALL

1   **Peach Brandy Wall (8)   P1:** Ascend the lower wall via easy cracks–many options. **P2:** (8) From the tree ledge, ascend cracks in the middle of the wall, well left of the roofs. **P3:** (8) Up the right-facing corner, passing a small roof.

2   **Peaches and Cream (10a) ★   P1:** Ascend the lower wall via easy cracks—many options. **P2:** (10a) Climb up to the roof, undercling left (pins), continue up the thin crack. **P3:** (8) Up the right-facing corner, passing a small roof.

SUPER CRACK SPIRE

3   **South Arête (6)**   Freelance up the low-angled, south-facing arête in two pitches of fun climbing. Rappel from fixed slings.

4   **Super Crack (9) ★**   Scramble up to a small right-facing corner. Up this, finishing on *South Arête*. Rappel from fixed slings.

5   **Regular Route (6)**   Climb the east face via flakes.

PEACH BRANDY WALL
1 Peach Brandy Wall (8)
2 Peaches and Cream (10a) ★
SUPER CRACK SPIRE
3 South Arête (6)
4 Super Crack (9) ★
5 Regular Route (6)

WARMUP WALL

From Newspaper Ledge, scramble through the notch, passing Super Crack Spire on your left.

6   **Warmup Route (9)**   Climb the low-angle face via a splitter crack; passing two small trees.

7   **Unknown (?)**   Located to the right of *Warmup Route* are many fixed pins and bolts. Not much is known about this route(s), except that with a good brushing they look as if they would be fun. They can be top-roped from the fixed anchor atop *Warmup Route*.

THE VIEW FROM
NEWSPAPER LEDGE

WARMUP WALL
6   Warmup Route (9)
7   Unknown (?)

WINDSONG WALL
8   Rollercoaster (10a R)
9   One Hand Scratching (10c)
10   Disappointment Dihedral (6)

WINDSONG WALL

From Newspaper Ledge, scramble through the notch, passing Super Crack Spire on your left and the Warmup Wall on your right. Descend by scrambling down the gully to the right of the wall.

8 **Rollercoaster (10a R)** Scramble up to the start which is the right side of a 30-foot pinnacle. **P1:** (9+) Climb the right side of the pinnacle. From the top of the pinnacle, move left and up, passing some fixed pro. Belay at a pine tree. **P2:** (10a) Straight up via a thin crack.

9 **One Hand Scratching (10c)** ★★ Climbs up a beautiful face located to the right of the *Rollercoaster* pinnacle. **P1:** (10c) Glide up the bolt-protected waterstreak to a fixed belay. Rappel or. . . **P2:** (10b) Continue up and left past three more bolts. Take a small rack.

10 **Disappointment Dihedral (6)** Looks great from afar, but the name says it all. Approach by scrambling in from the right, from the upper notch on the Castle Dome Trail. Or climb straight up to the dihedral via a 5.7 pitch. **P1:** (6) Climb the chimney.

UPPER INDIAN SPRINGS

From Newspaper Ledge, scramble through the notch, passing Super Crack Spire on your left. The routes are located uphill on your right. Routes are described from right to left as you walk up the hill.

11 **First Aid (10a)** ★ Actually located in the notch just beyond Newspaper Ledge, directly opposite Super Crack Spire. Climb past one bolt to the short jamcrack.

PIN CUSHION WALL

From Newspaper Ledge, scramble through the notch and turn right up the hill. You will immediately come to a low-angled face festooned with bolts. I lied when I said there was no sport-climbing in the Crags, here it is. The following routes have been supplemented by newer lines, making it hard to tell which route is which. However, with the exception of the second pitch of Snag, all routes are in the 5.9 - 10b range. Pick a line and connect the dots.

12 **Mild Steel (10b)** ★ Climb a short crack that leads to a bolt protected face. Find the anchor in a small alcove.

13 **Whisper (8)** Climb up a short ramp leads to cracks and flakes which are followed to the *Mild Steel* anchor.

14 **Psycho (9)** ★ Located just right of *Snag*. Follow five bolts to a belay alcove with a bush.

UPPER INDIAN SPRINGS
11   *First Aid (10a)* ★
PIN CUSHION WALL
12   *Mild Steel (10b)* ★
13   *Whisper (8)*
14   *Psycho (9)* ★
15   *Snag (11c)* ★

15   **Snag (11c)** ★   **P1:** (5.9) Climb a 5.9 crack, belay above the
        overhang. **P2:** (11c) Step left, climb up and right to the first of four
        bolts. Follow the bolts straight up to the top.

SIX TOE ROCK

Good routes on good rock.

APPROACH   *Starting in the state park Viewpoint parking lot, follow the
Castle Dome Trail for 2 miles until it turns from smooth dirt to rocky steps.
Continue up and winding around to a shoulder where you will pass through a
portal with rock walls on either side. At this point there will be a good view of
Castle Dome straight ahead. From this spot continue around to the left for a
hundred feet and look up and left through the trees where Six Toe Crack can
be seen. The climb is of high quality, better than it looks from the trail.
Bushwhack up through the trees and start at the base of the obvious crack in
the corner. Approach time: 60 minutes.*

Descent
Gully

.6

.7

.6 .7 .7

.9

.8

SIX TOE ROCK

16	Easy Street (6) ★
17	Easy On (7) ★
18	Six Toe Crack (8) ★★
19	Chocksucker (9) ★★
20	Purple Heart (8) ★

DESCENT   *All of the routes except Purple Heart merge at the top of Six Toe Crack. Rappel down Six Toe Crack. Or if you are brave, rap into the descent gully from the very top, from one bolt.*

16   **Easy Street (6)** ★   Two pitches of fun climbing on good rock follow the right-leaning crack on the far left side of the wall.

17   **Easy On (7)** ★   The obvious right-leaning crack that merges with *Six Toe Crack* at its midpoint.

18   **Six Toe Crack (8)** ★★ Ascends the obvious crack in the center of the face. Climb it in two or three pitches, belaying wherever you want. The crux comes early in the first pitch.

Six Toe Crack viewed from Castle Dome Trail.

19 **Chocksucker (9)** ★★ Start 30 feet right of *Six Toe Crack*, behind the large block at the base of the wall. Ascend the left-facing corner crack, staying just right of *Six Toe Crack*.

20 **Purple Heart (8)** ★ Follow *Chocksucker* half-way up the wall. Continue up and right to the arête and follow this to the summit.

THE MANSION, EAST FACE

The Mansion is located below the southwest face of Castle Dome, directly across from The Good Book. At press time there was only one established route on the formation, but there are more lines waiting to be climbed. There is no trail to The Mansion. It is reached by a short nasty bushwhack from the Castle Dome Trail.

APPROACH *Start in the State Park scenic overlook. Follow the Castle Dome Trail to Six Toe Rock. Continue past Six Toe Rock for 100 yards, then drop down to the right and traverse across brush-covered slabs. Locate a gully that drops down to the bottom of The Mansion. Approach time: 1.5 hours.*

DESCENT *No descent is required. An easy scramble and walk back and to the left brings you to the Castle Dome Trail.*

21 **Casino (11a)** ★★ A modern Crags classic courtesy of Peter Chesko and Tim Loughlin. Start in a cave, at the base of the east face. Standard rack. **P1:** (9) Exit the right side of the cave onto poor rock. Climb up the face onto better rock, passing two bolts to a fixed belay at a detached pinnacle. **P2:** (11a) Climb the steep face above via surreal stemming. Look for three bolts along the way. **P3:** (10a) Follow the dike with good pro and three more bolts. **P4:** Follow easy rock to the top.

4th

xx
③

x

x

②xx

x
x ⌐ 11a
x ⌐

detached
flake

①xx

.9

x

x

cave start

THE MANSION, EAST FACE
21   *Casino (11a)* ★★

3rd class

THE MANSION, EAST FACE

21   Casino (11a) ★★

walk off

easy

.9

.9+

.10d

.10a

.10b

.10c

.8

.9

22

23

24

25

Approach from Root Creek

CASTLE DOME, EAST FACE

22   East Face aka The Dike Route (10d) ★★★
23   The Good Book (10a) ★
24-25 Unknown (10)

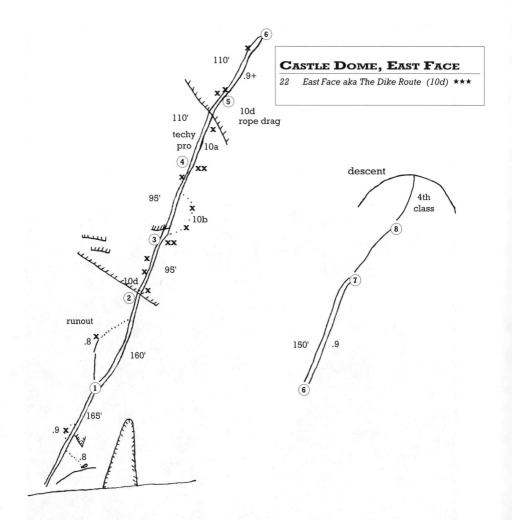

CASTLE DOME, EAST FACE	
22	*East Face aka The Dike Route (10d)* ★★★

CASTLE DOME, EAST FACE

APPROACH   *Start in the State Park scenic overlook. The east face is quite visible from there. Follow the Castle Dome Trail for a half-mile to the junction for the Root Creek trail. Follow the Root Creek trail for .75 mile at which point it ends along the left bank of the Root Creek. Continue by following the creekbed up and right for another mile to the base of the east face. Stay in the left fork of the creek bed if it's dry or, if it is wet, bushwhack through the woods, staying close to the creek. Allow 1.5 to 2 hours.*

An alternative approach is to follow the Castle Dome Trail all the way to base of the west (left) side, then scramble and rappel down a gully below the south facing slabs and contour around to the east face. This approach passes under The Good Book and might be wet in the early season. The easiest descent follows the Castle Dome Trail back to the park; don't plan on leaving any gear at the base of the route. Approach Time: 1.5 hours.

DESCENT *Scramble and walk off slabs to the southwest (left).*

22 **East Face aka The Dike Route (10d) ★★★** Standard rack to 3 inches with extra nuts and small cams. The East Face of Castle Dome is a sustained and technical climb that follows a diagonal dike up the longest part of the face. This route will challenge the experienced climber with a full range of objective difficulties. This adventure is not for everyone, but for those who are up to the challenge, the esthetic rewards are overwhelming. The route begins half way up the prominent ledge that extends across the bottom of the face. The start is on the left side of a small pillar and just below a downward pointing flake. The first bolt should be visible up and left of the flake. **P1:** (9) Climb up and left passing the flake on the way to a bolt. Follow the dike up and right to the belay, passing 1 more bolt. 165 feet. **P2:** (8) Leave the dike and follow a quartz seam up and left to a bolt and then angle up and right, returning to the dike. Belay below the roof. 160 feet. **P3:** (10c) Pull the roof and continue straight up the steep dike on good holds passing 2 more bolts. 90 feet. **P4:** (10b) Climb up and right to a bolt. Continue up to another bolt and then back left to the dike. Follow it to a 2 bolt belay. 95 feet. **P5:** (10d) From the belay climb straight up fractures and a groove, then move right to a stance and a bolt below the roof. Clip the bolt with a long runner, pull the roof and continue up and right to a 2 bolt belay. 110 feet. **P6:** (9+) Follow the dike for 100 feet of sustained climbing. **P7:** (5.9) Continue up the dike for another 150 feet of tricky climbing. **P8:** Easier climbing leads to the summit. Yahoo!

23 **The Good Book (10a) ★** *The Good Book* climbs up a huge left-facing corner on the south face of Castle Dome. **P1-P3:** The route can be climbed in two different styles: you can either thrash up the corner cracks direct; or climb up the face, staying 10-15 feet left of the crack.

24-25 **Unknown (10)** There are two more climbs immediately to the left of *The Good Book*. They are runout 5.10s. It may be possible to set up a top-rope from one of the belay stations of *The Good Book*.

Castle Dome, North and West Faces

26   *West Ridge (8)* ★
27   *North Face (10b)* ★

CASTLE DOME, NORTH AND WEST FACES

APPROACH   *Start in the State Park scenic overlook. Follow the Castle Dome Trail all the way to the base of the west (left) side of Castle Dome. Continue by descending into the ravine below the observation deck. Rope up at the large fir tree. Approach time: 1.5 hours.*

DESCENT   *Scramble and walk off slabs to the south (right).*

26   **West Ridge (8)** ★   Some loose rock. The objective challenges come from exposure, natural protection and route finding rather than from sustained climbing. Views of Mt. Shasta and the surrounding Crags are breathtaking. To start - descend into the ravine below the observation deck. Rope up at the large fir tree. Standard rack to 2.5 inches. **P1:** (5.8) The route begins directly across from the tree, well to the left of the actual west ridge, on low angled rock at a small dike. Climb up the dike to a small ledge and belay at a small tree. **P2:** (5.7) Continue straight up via tricky face climbing to the point where the face steepens and then traverse right to a good stance on the large ledge. **P3:** (5.2) Continue right across the "No Reverse Traverse" being careful of loose rock and belay below a detached flake. **P4:** (5.8) Climb the "Potato Chip Flake" and continue straight up to a belay ledge. Don't be the one to pull the flake off. **P5:** (5.8) Move up and left to a groove and climb straight up past two ancient bolts with piton hangers; ending at a good belay ledge. **P6:** (5.5) Easier climbing leads to the summit.

CASTLE DOME, WEST FACE

26   West Ridge (8)
     ★

27   **North Face (10b)** ★   The sixth pitch goes free at 10b or can be negotiated via an easy pendulum. To start, descend into the ravine below the observation deck. Rope up at the large fir tree. The first pitch is shared with the *West Ridge* route. There are many ways to get to the start of the fourth pitch. The story of the first ascent by Lincoln Freese in the 1977 American Alpine Journal describes the original route. The following description and topo map describe the more common variation. It is also possible to descend to the very bottom of the face and climb an additional two or three easy pitches to get to the start. Standard rack to three inches. **P1:** (5.8) The route begins directly across from the tree, well to the left of the actual west ridge, on low-angled rock at a small dike. Climb up the dike and face to a small ledge and belay at a small tree. **P2:** (5.9) Climb up and right to a left-facing corner. Up the corner to a long ledge. **P3:** (5.7) Avoid the ugly crack above by traversing left to the end of the ledge. Climb up the face to another ledge. **P4:** (5.7) Traverse right and the ascend a jamcrack to a good stance and the beginning of a left-facing corner. **P5:** (5.9) Ascend the jamcrack in the left-facing corner until it's possible to traverse left to the bush-covered ledge. **P6:** (10b) Climb 25 feet up the pinnacle to the slings. Traverse left to the ramp and easier climbing. Belay at the high point of the ramp. **P7:** (5.9) Finish by pinching crystals on the steep black face.

top

.9
dike

⑥

10b

⑤

.9

④

.7

③ →

.7

②

.9

①

.8

CASTLE DOME, NORTH FACE	
27	North Face (10b) ★

The author heads up Potato Chip Flake, Castle Dome, West Ridge (5.8) ★

ROOT CREEK

28   *Dike Hike (8)* ★★
29   *Dunsmuir Avenue (10c)*

ROOT CREEK

APPROACH   *Start in the State Park scenic overlook. Follow the Castle Dome Trail all the way to the base of the west (left) side of Castle Dome. Continue up and left (west) past two mini-domes. From the ridge, look to the northeast (right) and locate the Dike Hike in the distance. Descend by bushwhacking into Root Creek. Approach time: 2.5 hours.*

DESCENT   *Scramble left to the top of Dunsmuir Avenue and continue down via slabs to the left(west).*

28   **Dike Hike (8)** ★★   Approach by scrambling up the talus at the base of the spine. **P1:** (5.4) Easy climbing leads up to a roof on the right side of the dike. **P2:** (5.8) Move right around the roof and then up the dike. **P3:** (5.4) Climb to the top of the formation.

29   **Dunsmuir Avenue (10c)**   **P1:** (5.8) From the bottom of the buttress, climb straight up via a dike. Belay at a bolt on the left edge of a roof. **P2:** (5.9) Continue up a right-facing corner, pass a bolt, and then move left onto the large ledge system. **P3:** (5.7) From the left end of the ledge, climb a chimney to a tree. **P4:** (10c) Continue up the corner to a ledge. **P5:** Easy climbing leads to the top.

MT. HUBRIS (THE OGRE)

The Ogre is situated a quarter-mile west of Castle Dome and is easily distinguished by the fractured rock on its south face that forms the face of an ogre. The Ogre is comprised of excellent rock and these routes are some of the best in the park.

APPROACH   *Starting in the state park Viewpoint parking lot, follow the Castle Dome Trail all the way to the south (left) side of Castle Dome. Angle up and left on the ridgeline on faint trails through the scrub, finally dropping down to the base of the south face of The Ogre. Approach time: 1.5 to 2 hours.*

DESCENT   *Two rappels down the northeast side take you to a gully where it is easy to scramble down and back to the approach trail. Either two ropes or a 60-meter rope is required for the first rap.*

30   **Golden Opportunity (9)** ★   Start on the far right side of the south face. **P1:** (5.7 R) Face climb up to a small tree. **P2:** (5.9) Up the steep face via flakes to a terrace, then move left to another tree. P3-5. Continue up and left via easy terrain, merging with *Cosmic Wall.*

31   **Cosmic Wall (6)** ★★★   Low-angled face climb that goes up the right side of the face. First climbed in 1979, the route is a classic featuring solid rock, straight forward route finding, adequate

protection and a small airy summit. Start at the base of a large pine tree, at the base of a large right-facing corner. Cams are more useful than nuts. **P1:** Climb the corner past a tree and continue straight up to belay on a good ledge with a small tree (1 or 2 pitches). **P2:** Continue up and right on fractured rock until able to step right onto a small ledge to a belay with a small tree. **P3:** Continue straight up for 100 feet to a two-bolt belay stance. **P4:** Continue straight up to a large ledge and a belay. **P5:** Climb up and right for a full rope length. Belay in the notch. **P6:** The final pitch traverses left for 20 feet and then follows a low-angle chimney up and right to the summit.

32   **Faceted Dike (10b)** ★   Start as for *Cosmic Wall*, but climb straight up through The Ogre's left nostril (climber's right). Follow the faceted dike straight up, eventually finishing on the last two pitches of *Cosmic Wall*.

33   **Solar Wind (10d)** ★★★   *Solar Wind* follows weaknesses up the center of the face through the nose and The Ogre's right eye. Start 100 feet left of *Cosmic Wall*. Standard rack from RPs to 3.5 inches with extra cams in the .5 to 1.5 inch range. **P1:** (5.7) Scramble up the face for 200+ feet to a ledge and belay below the nose. **P2:** (10d) Climb straight up past three bolts and two roofs to a two-bolt belay, 165 feet. **P3:** (10a) Follow the dike up and step right (10a) and continue up on quartz rock to a two-bolt belay, 165 feet. **P4:** Wander up and right past a bolt and a sugar pine to the *Cosmic Wall* notch (5.9+). **P5:** The final pitch traverses left for 20 feet and then follows a low-angle chimney up and right to the summit.

34   **The Great Chimney (8)**   Three or four direct pitches up the obvious chimney.

MT. HUBRIS (THE OGRE)

30	Golden Opportunity (9) ★
31	Cosmic Wall (6) ★★★
32	Faceted Dike (10b) ★
33	Solar Wind (10d) ★★★
34	The Great Chimney (8)

two 100'
rappels

.9+
.6
10a.
165'
.5
.5
10b
10b
.9
belay
.8
.6
32
165'
31
.7R
30
.7
.4
200'
180'
34
33

Diane Wilson on Cosmic Wall (5.6) ★★★

INDEX

Bolded numbers refer to either topos, maps or photos of the route; rock features are listed in all capitals.

ACCESS: It's every climber's concern

The Access Fund, a national, non-profit climbers organization, works to keep climbing areas open and to conserve the climbing environment. Need help with closures? land acquisition? legal or land management issues? funding for trails and other projects? starting a local climbers' group? CALL US!

Climbers can help preserve access by being committed to Leave No Trace (minimum-impact) practices. Here are some simple guidelines:

• **ASPIRE TO "LEAVE NO TRACE"** especially in environmentally sensitive areas like caves. Chalk can be a significant impact on dark and porous rock – don't use it around historic rock art. Pick up litter, and leave trees and plants intact.

• **DISPOSE OF HUMAN WASTE PROPERLY** Use toilets whenever possible. If toilets are not available, dig a "cat hole" at least six inches deep and 200 feet from any water, trails, campsites, or the base of climbs. *Always pack out toilet paper.* On big wall routes, use a "poop tube" and carry waste up and off with you (the old "bag toss" is now illegal in many areas).

• **USE EXISTING TRAILS** Cutting switchbacks causes erosion. When walking off-trail, tread lightly, especially in the desert where cryptogamic soils (usually a dark crust) take thousands of years to form and are easily damaged. Be aware that "rim ecologies" (the clifftop) are often highly sensitive to disturbance.

• **BE DISCRETE WITH FIXED ANCHORS** *Bolts are controversial and are not a convenience*—don't place 'em unless they are *really* necessary. Camouflage all anchors. Remove unsightly slings from rappel stations (better to use steel chain or welded cold shuts). Bolts sometimes can be used proactively to protect fragile resources—consult with your local land manager.

• **RESPECT THE RULES** and speak up when other climbers don't. Expect restrictions in designated wilderness areas, rock art sites, caves, and to protect wildlife, especially nesting birds of prey. *Power drills are illegal in wilderness and all national parks.*

• **PARK AND CAMP IN DESIGNATED AREAS** Some climbing areas require a permit for overnight camping.

• **MAINTAIN A LOW PROFILE** Leave the boom box and day-glo clothing at home— the less climbers are heard and seen, the better.

• **RESPECT PRIVATE PROPERTY** Be courteous to land owners. Don't climb where you're not wanted.

• **JOIN THE ACCESS FUND** Become a member! Make a tax-deductible donation of $25.

The Access Fund

Preserving America's Diverse Climbing Resources
PO Box 17010
Boulder, CO 80308
303.545.6772 • www.accessfund.org